Sales Wisdom from a Toilet Paper Salesman

Sales Wisdom from a Toilet Paper Salesman

A Handbook for B2B Sales, Sales Management, Leadership and Life Success

Michael Mirarchi

ISBN 10: 0692732896
ISBN 13: 9780692732892
Library of Congress Control Number: 2016906057
CreateSpace Independent Publishing Platform
North Charleston, South Carolina

Contents

ACKNOWLEDGMENTS

Thanks to God, who sustains me daily. He is the reason I have any success in sales at all, and even though I am far from perfect, he loves me just the same.

I was raised by two parents who have touched so many lives through their service to others. My pop, Frank, passed on in 2012. My mom, Toni, is still here. I'm so excited for her to see this book. So much of who I am is because of them, and I thank them from the bottom of my heart.

I would like to thank my wife, Christine, who is a talented artist and a very supportive wife and mother. She is my counterbalance. She was instrumental in making this book happen and contributed in editing much of it. I love her more today than the day we were married.

We've had the privilege of raising two amazing kids, Liz and Dave. Liz is an artist, writer, and businessperson. David is a jazz musician, composer, and entrepreneur. Christine and I are both very proud of who they have become. I appreciate their support.

Thanks to all of the dedicated people at Huff United who have helped make my success possible. Phil, Skip, Bob, Paul, Fred, Kathy B., Mark, Jim G. Bill B. Josie, Kathy K., Michelle, Terri, Leslie, Barb, Chris, Debbie, Nancy, The warehouse Bill D., Tim, Martin, Robert, Chris, Tony, John, Michael, Dennis, Steve, Edward, Joseph, Tony, Ed, and the drivers

Alonzo, Mike, Brian, Art, and Horez. Without their hard work and dedication making sales would be much more difficult.

I would like to thank Adam Grundt, Corey Iyoob, and Kevin Iyoob. I had the privilege of leading them in a confirmation class this year in 2016. We learned together to follow the path God has set for us. I expect great things from them.

I would also like to thank Mike Bouselli, who has been a student of mine for many years and who has written the foreword to this book. He is a person who is always ready to learn and willing to listen. He has encouraged me for years to reach further, and I value his friendship.

Finally, I would like to thank all the people at CreateSpace who helped make this book possible. They have been great to work with and have made the whole publishing process easy. If you are considering self-publishing, I would recommend them highly.

Foreword

"That's a stupid price!" Those were some of the first words uttered to me by Mike Mirarchi after I told him his competitor's price was a lot lower than his. That was over twenty-two years ago. I had just started my first sales job selling restaurant supplies at a small mom-and-pop dealer. Mike was our redistributor salesman, and he would come in like clockwork every Friday morning at 10:00 a.m. Mike was only a year older than me, but he was already a polished salesman in his own right.

I had been working as a carpenter and delivery person for ten years before I took a job in sales. At the time, I had no idea how to sell anything or that my life would be positively influenced by Mike over the coming years, as it is still being influenced today.

Mike has been my mentor, teacher, and sometimes my psychiatrist over the last couple of decades. His teachings have inspired me to be a successful salesman with over twenty years of continuous sales growth. I have since moved on to a larger firm. Today, not only have I been the top salesperson in my company for the last fourteen years, but I am also one of the top salespeople in my market segment.

Mike's timeless analogies on sales in *Sales Wisdom from a Toilet-Paper Salesman* will help any person, be it someone just starting out in sales or a seasoned veteran who is looking for inspiration. From the "Apple

Picker" to "Selling Profitably," Mike explains how to get new customers, increase profits, and maintain good customer relations for years to come.

"Sales Wisdom from a Toilet Paper Salesman" is a must read for any new sales person and should be given to any new hire as a sales training tool.

Michael J. Bouselli

INTRODUCTION

After more than thirty years of successfully selling toilet paper (among other things) to the wholesale trade, opening hundreds of new accounts, creating new territories from scratch, growing sales dramatically, and training many sales teams, I have decided to share what I have learned about success in a plain and concise manner. This practical guidance and no-nonsense approach is a welcome departure from the old way of selling.

In this book, I share my wisdom and methods, which will help any salesperson be more successful in sales, management, and life.

Success is a journey; we get better step by step, moment by moment. Even though it seems like we make large strides, many times it is only after going through a plateau. If we are growing, we take thousands of these steps throughout our lifetime. Unfortunately, most people find one of those comfortable plateaus and stay there for a long period of time. What they don't realize is that life's plateaus aren't flat; they are on a slight upgrade. If you are not moving forward, then you are moving backward. People reach a certain place and think, "I've hit my stride; this is a good place," so they unpack and settle on the plateau. When this happens, they turn on their autopilot without realizing it and start living life like pages in a book. The years flip by, and they realize at some point that they wasted a good portion of their precious gift of life. With much regret, many pass on, wishing they had done more, lived more, and accomplished more. It's such a shame that so many people live an existence and not a life. It's very sad that their talent is wasted and untapped, their dreams are unfulfilled, and they accept mediocrity as their reality. The good news is that you can pack up and move from the plateau you're on and continue your life's journey of growth. You need only to turn off your autopilot, start thinking about the things you would like to accomplish in your life, and then take small steps toward your dream.

As I developed and facilitated the Sales Wisdom training program, many people told me I should write a book. I wanted to, but life just kept passing by, and ten years later nothing was written. Then one day I read a sales article on LinkedIn with which I disagreed. As I started to write a comment stating my disagreement, I said to myself, "Instead of commenting on this article, I can write an article myself." So I did. Because my grammar isn't the best, my wife, Chris, who was a French major in college, edited my article, and I posted it. After receiving good feedback, I wrote another. For the next year and a half, I wrote articles whenever an idea would pop into my head. Then I stopped getting ideas. For about three months, I didn't have a single idea for an article. I was getting really down about it because I thought I had stopped moving forward. Then on an airplane ride home from Detroit, I began thinking about writing a book. I thought, "I have a bunch of PowerPoint presentations. I could hire a ghost writer—ah no, that would cost too much, and besides, who would I get?" Then it hit me like a ton of bricks. Over the past year and a half, I had written thirty-eight articles—I already had the book mostly written! I immediately went to work on the flight, organizing the articles into chapters, and I came up with thirty. Just by taking small actions on a regular basis, I almost wrote an entire book in a year and a half without realizing it. When I made the decision to take action and start writing articles, I packed up my mind and started on my journey to write this book.

My hope is that this book inspires you to pack up, get off your plateau, start moving forward, and take the next step to a fruitful and successful career and life. I hope you enjoy the book and would love your feedback.

Mike Mirarchi
mikemirarchi23@gmail.com
April 2016

CHAPTER 1

Wanted: People of Integrity at Every Level

The strength of a nation derives from the integrity of the home.
—Confucius

I lost my father in 2012. He had served in World War II, was a dedicated husband and father, and would give the shirt off his back to anyone who asked. I remember countless times when he would lend a hand to someone in need. From taking care of his bedridden father who had tuberculosis to bringing people who needed a hand into our house to mowing lawns, changing tires, and doing every other kind of good deed, my dad was always willing to help. No matter what the cost, he was there, and he never asked for anything in return. He was selfless in every way, and he died a very rich man. If judged by our current society, he would not have been deemed "successful" because he didn't have material wealth. He didn't buy and sell companies or have billions of dollars or play professional sports like the people we uphold as role models today. He was an honest and humble man who made a difference in people's lives every day. He was the embodiment of the greatest generation.

Like my father, the men and women of his generation are slowly dying and will soon be gone. Who will fill the void? We have many leaders today, but by title *only*, because their integrity is absent. Even at the highest levels, we see examples of people in positions of leadership with not a shred of integrity, setting terrible examples of what a leader should be.

The God-fearing men and women of the greatest generation were no different from you or me. One trait they possessed that set them apart was selflessness; they gave everything to help one another and their country. They always put the interests of others first and didn't have the "What's in it for me?" attitude. They mentored, developed, and inspired people to greatness.

Now it's our turn to step up to the plate. Throughout our lives, each one of us will be a leader of something. Whether it is leading our families, our companies, or our friends, we are setting examples and leading. Although some people are born leaders, the rest of us must acquire the skills. It isn't done by reading a book or attending a seminar: it takes a commitment to become the best person you can be, to put others first, to live a life of integrity, and to become a great example for the next generation to follow. We must take responsibility to lead the next generation into the future. Will you join me in accepting the challenge?

CHAPTER 2

The Best Coach I've Ever Had

The secret of our success is that we never, never give up.
—Wilma Mankiller

When I was a kid, I wanted to play peewee football. I remember that my parents were unenthusiastic about my participation and for good reason: I was young and very small. I was probably the smallest guy in the league. After much pestering, they finally let me play.

I was excited to play because a lot of my friends did, but I had big shoes to fill. My older brother was an excellent player. He was fearless, tough, and hard-nosed.

My coaches assumed that I would be as good as he was. The head coach, Coach Bright, seemed like he was ten feet tall. He was loud and tough and expected excellence. In the beginning he was very intimidating. What I discovered was that he was a great leader.

The fact that my brother was so good did afford me some privileges. I played with the first-team defense as an outside linebacker. When they discovered that I couldn't tackle, I was demoted to second team.

The next thing I knew, I was called over to a separate group. Coach Henderson announced that I was on the "scrub squad." He was in charge of turning us scrubs into football players. I don't remember being disappointed, because deep down I knew he was right. In fact, I was somewhat relieved because I no longer had to live up to the expectations that were set by my brother.

I then found out I would be playing on the offensive line as a guard. Most small players don't play on the line, but I was happy to accept my new assignment. I got my playbook and was excited to learn it. I started practicing with the line, and before long I was playing on the first team.

After every practice and before and after each game we had a chant: "*We never give up, we never give up*!" We chanted before our first game, and I went out on the field as the starting right guard. I was called for a clipping penalty early in the game. I don't know what the coaches thought, but they were probably just glad I hit somebody. They didn't yell at me; they encouraged me. I didn't have a penalty the rest of the season.

I liked my new position, and the coaches must have been happy because I remained the starter. The game during which I realized I was getting pretty good was when we ran the same play for the whole of the second half of a game. It was called "the dive." The play was to hand the fullback the ball and run right up the middle. Because I was a guard, I was one of the main blockers on the play. It worked so well that the fullback gained eight to ten yards every play, and the other team couldn't stop us. It was the greatest feeling to be a big part of our team's success.

We won the championship that year. It wasn't because we had the most talented or the biggest players; it was because we had the best coach. Coach Bright inspired us to reach our fullest potential. He took his worst players and made them an asset. He taught us how to work hard, play as a team, and always do our best. Most importantly, he taught us to *never give up*!

This one lesson has served me well through the years. The only true loser is the one who gives up.

The art of great leadership is understanding your team members' strengths and weaknesses and finding a place where they will excel and then inspiring them to be their best. Investing time and resources into this goal will pay big dividends, and it will create happy and motivated employees.

CHAPTER 3

WHAT IS SUCCESS?

What we have done for ourselves alone dies with us; what we have done for others and the world remains and is immortal.
—ALBERT PIKE

We recently moved and had the task of cleaning out of our house all of the stuff we had accumulated while our kids were growing up. We were astounded by how much we had amassed over the years, and it was a pleasure to pare it down and transition into a new phase in our lives.

After our daughter graduated college and was on her own and our son left for college, we were left with an empty house. The realization hit us that our kids were never really ours. They were given to us for eighteen years to raise and then to mentor. What an honor to be able to guide our kids through the trials of life and watch them grow into amazing and productive adults.

It raised the question of what we actually own. The ownership of stuff is really a myth. The simple reality is that someday we will all pass away and then we will own nothing. All of our possessions will be passed on to others.

What we do with our most precious possession of is entirely up to us. Many talk about long-term goals and dreams, which are beneficial to have, but aren't most important. Each day we should have one goal: How do I make the most of the gift of this day?

The measure of a successful life is not how much we acquire but how much we give. When we're gone, no one will really care how much money we made or how many businesses, cars, boats, or houses we owned. What will remain is how many people we touched, how many lives we changed, and how much we gave back.

Each new day is an opportunity to be a wealth maker or a wealth spreader. Which will you choose?

CHAPTER 4

Seven Resolutions to Success

The starting point of all achievement is desire.
—Napoleon Hill

New Year's is a time when resolutions are made and then broken shortly afterward. We don't have to wait until the new year to make changes in our lives. This chapter offers seven simple resolutions that will give you the biggest bang for your buck. If you can make a small improvement in each of these areas, you will not only be much happier, but you will also become a better person.

1. Resolve to *really* listen.

Today, we are so frequently distracted that we often only give part of our attention to the people with whom we spend our time. If you listen intently, not only will you learn something, but also those with whom you are speaking will appreciate being heard.

2. Resolve to ask more questions.

We have a tendency to talk more than listen and to "tell" more than ask. When you "tell," you can't learn; when you ask, you are open to learning something new.

3. Resolve to expand your comfort zone.
When you are comfortable, you are not growing as a person. In order to grow, you must try new things. An easy way to get started is to make a bucket list. Include not only big items on your list but also small things like trying a new food or traveling to a new place. Try sitting in a different seat on the train, or try a new restaurant. Also be willing to add to the list as you go. If you are at a restaurant and you have a chance to try something new, go for it! You will find that these small changes make a difference, and your life will be much richer for it.

4. Resolve to spend more time with your family.
As technology advances, it is getting harder to separate our work life from our personal life. The result is that we aren't really home even when we are physically there. Turn off your electronic devices at mealtimes and after a certain time at night. Your family will appreciate it.

5. Resolve to get to know someone you don't like.
Abraham Lincoln said, "I don't like that man. I need to get to know him better." Many times when we don't like someone it is because we don't truly know him or her. Resolve to get to know the individual and do everything you can to make things right. If you can turn a negative relationship into a positive one, it will make your life much better.

6. Resolve to randomly do something nice for someone.
Every day you have a chance to make a difference in someone's life, whether it is by smiling at someone, giving someone a big tip, or helping someone in need. There are times when we are uncertain if we should act. Should I tip in this situation? Should I help? Anytime you have this conflict, decide to act. If you have a thought about doing a good deed, just do it—don't talk yourself out of it. Many times you will find that a small deed will make a big difference in a person's day or life.

7. Resolve to have an attitude of gratitude.

Each day, look for opportunities to be thankful for everything that is good in your life. When you are faced with negatives, turn them into opportunities. If you view a negative as an opportunity, it will help you stay positive and handle the situation better. Look at negatives as an opportunity to learn something new or deal with a new circumstance. When someone does something nice for you, thank him or her by sending a handwritten note or a small gift. You can't feel gratitude and anger at the same time, so choose gratitude. You will be much happier and enjoy your life much more.

Today, you have an opportunity to start fresh and do better. There is nothing you can do to change the past, but you can make a difference today, tomorrow, and in the future. Resolve to make these changes. If you fail one day, you will have the next day. Don't worry about hitting home runs; a single is fine. If you can do one of these items once a week, it will make a difference. Resolve to make a difference; your family, coworkers, and friends will be glad you did.

CHAPTER 5

Be Successful by Doing Zero

Helping others isn't a chore; it is one of the greatest gifts there is.
—Liya Kebede

One day as I checked in for a dentist appointment, the assistant, Chrissy, informed me that Doc was in the hospital. As we were talking, Chrissy said she got zero done yesterday. She said, "I spent the whole day with Doc and then ran errands for him, and at the end of the day, I was so exhausted that I couldn't do anything else."

Then it hit me. I told her that she actually did a lot yesterday. Spending the whole day with Doc was a big deal and was the most important thing she could have done. I could see the relief on her face. She was thinking that she had accomplished nothing.

Just a week later, Doc passed, which made her day with him that much more important.

I realized how many times I feel the same way. In this age of working longer and longer hours, I find myself feeling guilty when I'm not working no matter if it is during the evening, on weekends, or even on vacation. This is the wrong mind-set. A day doing absolutely nothing is just as meaningful as a long, productive day at work. We must take time to rest and recharge our batteries. Spending time with your family, or a sick friend, is getting something very important done.

If spending time with your family, a day with a sick friend, or a day to rest is doing zero, then we need to be doing zero more often. Resolve today to stop feeling guilty. You will find that when you are working you will be much more productive. In addition, you will feel better and be healthier, and your family and friends will thank you for it.

CHAPTER 6

What Are We Willing to Sacrifice?

There is no decision that we can make that doesn't come with some sort of balance or sacrifice.
—Simon Sinek

At some point in our lives, we are faced with decisions that alter the course of our careers.

These decisions are forks in the road; they can mean the difference between being very successful career-wise, staying the same, or taking a step backward.

From a business standpoint these decisions seem easy, but many times there is a price for career advancement.

What are we willing to sacrifice for career advancement and material gain?

Many marriages have been destroyed and families broken apart by career moves.

Who do you think will have had more success at the end of their lives?

Those who made it to the top and in their wake left behind broken marriages and resentful kids, all for the sake of success?

OR

Those who gave up the corner office or flying a million miles a year for the sake of their families?

Our society has been fed a bunch of garbage for a long time about what it is to be a success, and we have bought it hook, line, and sinker. We have been told that "we can have it all." Just look at what we are left with: a 50 percent divorce rate, kids who are lost, and a society that is breaking down.

Our holidays have been turned into shopping sprees to promote huge sales, with people camping outside stores for days so that they can be first to get bargain prices. Each year people get trampled just to save a few hundred dollars on a fancy new big-screen TV! How misguided is that?

We don't take vacations anymore, and when we do, we are working as much as if we were in the office. On this one, I am guilty as charged.

Is it really worth the sacrifice? What is the price of having made it to the top, and what is the cost of getting there? Only you can answer these questions.

CHAPTER 7

Do You Want to Make a Difference?

> Your big opportunity may be right where you are now.
>
> —Napoleon Hill

I was talking with a friend about our kids, and he told me his son was considering joining the military. When I asked him why, he said, "He wants to make a difference." Although I believe it is very honorable to want to serve one's country, I couldn't help thinking that that isn't the only way to make a difference. Making a difference isn't a homerun thing; it is a daily living thing. We have the opportunity to make a difference every single day with every person we touch. We truly have no idea how we influence people's lives just by how we interact with them.

Many times we fall into the trap of thinking that if we could only get a promotion, or if we could make more money, or if we lived under different circumstances, or if we joined the military, we could then make a real difference. Don't miss opportunities to make a difference where you are right now. If you commit to making a difference each day, you will be on your way to making a cumulative difference throughout your life that will yield big results. It's like systematic savings: it starts out small, and then one day you realize how much you have accumulated. The best part is that we all get a new chance to make a difference every day.

CHAPTER 8

SUCCESS: IT'S ALL ABOUT THE PEOPLE

Your success in life is a direct reflection on how you treat each person you come in contact with daily.
—MICHAEL MIRARCHI

I have heard it said that "the world is a great place if not for the people." Newsflash—the world is the people!

Every day we interact with many people. How do we make them feel? Do we leave them feeling good about themselves, are you indifferent, or do you make them feel like dirt?

I was on a sales call for a large account with one of my Salespeople. During the call, the VP of purchasing continually belittled the buyer about a mistake that was made. It was awkward and embarrassing. The buyer had done exactly what the VP asked her to do, and the VP made a big deal of blaming it on the buyer, essentially saying she was incompetent.

At that point, does it really matter if this person is a VP? Does it matter how much money she makes? Does it matter what kind of car she drives or how big her house is? No. What matters is how she treats those she leads and those she deals with every day.

We are on this earth for a very short time, and at the end our lives we will be remembered by how we treated the people we were in contact with each day. No matter your material status in life, you will be a giant success if you treat people well. Make them feel special and valuable. No matter how much material wealth you have accumulated, you will have failed if you treat people badly.

Try an experiment. For one day, treat everyone you meet like they are the most important people in the world and observe what happens. You will be amazed at the difference it makes not only for them but also for yourself.

When you are able to live life off autopilot and start focusing on helping and loving others, this is the top level of success. It's my hope that this book will help you in some way to get started on your journey.

CHAPTER 9

The Most Important Lesson I Learned from My Mentor

The snow goose need not bathe to make itself white.
Neither need you do anything but be yourself.
—Lao Tzu

As I was getting ready to graduate college with an associate's degree in hotel restaurant management, my goal was to start my career with a food-service management company and then to own my own restaurant. I had the opportunity to go to a four-year college program, but because I financed my own education, I couldn't afford it.

One day at the end of my final year, I was asked to consider interviewing for a sales position for Maid Rite Steak Company. Being a salesperson was the furthest thing from my mind. The vision I had of a salesperson was someone going door-to-door selling vacuum cleaners. As a child, I never sold candy or participated in fundraisers. I was afraid to knock on someone's door to sell something; it was embarrassing.

My father worked in a factory as a punch press operator, and both of my brothers, neither of whom went to college, worked at the same factory with my father. I remember sitting at the dinner table when I was a teenager and making the following statement: "I will never work in a factory. I'm going to work with a suit and tie on each day." There is nothing wrong with working in a factory or any other manual labor, but it just wasn't for me.

I decided to interview for the position despite not being interested in sales because it would be a good chance to hone my interviewing skills.

However, as I learned more about the opportunity during the interview, I became very interested. The interview went well enough that I was invited back for a second one, where I was given a plant tour and met the owner of the company, Mr. Bernstein. He was very nice, and I was very interested. After the interview, I was at home watching TV when it hit me that I needed to write a thank-you note. I sat down and wrote the note by hand, expressing my interest and letting Mr. Bernstein know that I thought I could do a good job. A few weeks later, I received a phone call from Mr. Bernstein and was offered the position. I later learned that one of the reasons I got the position is that I was the only candidate to write a thank-you note. At nineteen years old, I was on my way to my first assignment as a portion control meat specialist in Syracuse, New York, to meet the national sales manager.

When I met Gerry, the national sales manager, it was clear that he was very different from anyone I had known before. The best way I can describe him is as a human resources nightmare. He broke every rule in the book, and political correctness was not his strong suit. Gerry used just about every foul word in the English language early and often. He had the ability to be completely wrong and be so convincing that he had the other party not only admitting they were wrong but actually apologizing, even with overwhelming evidence against him. It was an eye-opening experience, to say the least. Gerry was a very effective old-school salesperson, and he was now my mentor.

I learned a lot from my mentor. He taught me to, in his words, "Walk, talk, eat, and sh**." It became obvious that I couldn't sell like he did. Fortunately, he was so unorthodox in his methods that it was impossible to emulate him without getting fired.

I can tell you this because I tried and should have lost my job. Once, I was assigned to go to a trade show in Ohio to represent the company. I was new and young and had learned from Gerry; being naïve, I acted with complete disrespect to the company, the owners, and the customers. I made a fool of myself and gave a terrible impression of the company. A week or so later, I was called into Mr. Bernstein's office on a Sunday evening. I wasn't sure why he called, but I knew it was something big. Mr. Bernstein got a call from the customer complaining about my attitude and stating that they never wanted to have me at their show again. He gave me a stern talking to, and I still don't know why I didn't get fired that evening. My guess is that Gerry bailed me out. I learned a very valuable lesson that day and never acted like that again.

There were many lessons I learned from Gerry that I still use to this day. He was an excellent salesperson and had a wealth of knowledge. He dominated the market and was very hard to compete against. He taught me a lot about sales, salesmanship, and winning. I owe a lot to Gerry.

The most important lesson I learned from Gerry is that you have to be yourself and sell the way you are comfortable with. When you are trying to be someone you're not, it's like the guy who is wearing a bad hairpiece. It makes him feel better and may give him more confidence, but it sticks out like a sore thumb. People notice when you are trying to be someone you're not, and it always leaves a negative impression. Let the real you shine through—you will be much happier, and it will set the course for a successful future.

CHAPTER 10

Off to Huff Paper

"An investment in knowledge pays the best interest."
—Benjamin Franklin

I spent almost three years at Maid Rite, but the traveling was rough. Each week, I left on Sunday night and returned on Thursday. I met my future wife at Maid Rite, and it was then that I decided I needed a position with less overnight travel. A friend from college suggested that I apply at the company where he worked, Marstan Industries, selling restaurant supplies and equipment to restaurants, hospitals, nursing homes, colleges, and the like. The company was very leery about hiring me as they were just moving on from a young rep who had done a terrible job. I interviewed with Stu Cohen, and he was impressed enough with me that he recommended they give me a shot, which they did. I started with Marstan with little knowledge of restaurant supplies and equipment other than using them at the various restaurant jobs I had worked at during high school and college. I started out on fire, opening at least twenty accounts with ease in my first few months and by the end of the year I was up 30 percent. For the next two years, I continued with 30 percent increases each year. However, the company kept changing the compensation plan, and I made less money in my third year than in the year before, even after being up 30 percent. That was the end for me; I decided I needed a change.

An Interview at Huff Paper

A few months later, I saw an ad in a trade magazine for a district sales manager's job. I called the recruiter and inquired about the position. The recruiter told me she didn't think the job was right for me, but she had a different position with a company called Huff Paper. Huff is a redistributor of food service, institutional paper, and janitorial supplies. The company sells to wholesalers who resale to restaurants, hospitals, and other end-user accounts. I knew about Huff because we competed for a few wholesale accounts. They had a very good reputation, and I was interested. I remember the interview like it was yesterday. I arrived at the bottom of the stairs to the office, and standing at the top was the company president, Phil Sullivan. It was a great interview. I felt very comfortable with Phil, and everyone at the company seemed really nice. I was offered the position and started a new chapter in my life.

Mike Who?

In March 1988, I started my career with Huff Paper. After a few weeks of training, I was at the car dealership picking up my company car. My wife, Chris, took a picture of me in my new ride, and I was off to New Jersey to make sales calls. It was my first day on the road, and I didn't even know where I was going. I pulled off an exit and saw a new prospective account. I stopped by and introduced myself. We talked about what Huff had to offer. I was fumbling around as the customer asked me about some of the products we had available. The customer must have felt bad for me because at the end of our conversation I got an order. I was very excited so I called the office and asked for Phil. When they told Phil I was on the phone, Phil said, "Mike? Mike who?" It stuck, and for many years I was known as Mike Who.

Huff Paper was a much different company than Marstan. Marstan was huge for the times, at about $125 million, whereas Huff was much smaller. Marstan had what seemed like a football field of employees working in the office, whereas Huff had only a handful. Huff is a family, and I absolutely love the company, which is why I'm still here to this day.

Phil was an amazing leader to work for. He knew exactly how to get the most out of me, and the results were amazing. I grew 30 percent each year for the next twelve years, opening five new territories and hundreds of new accounts.

I spent my first year at Huff in northern New Jersey, after which I took over the northeastern Pennsylvania and Binghamton, New York, markets. After about a year, I wanted to open Syracuse, New York, so each time I was at the Huff office I would ask Bob Ward, who was another owner in charge of logistics and the warehouse, about this possibility. Each time he said, "No, we're not ready yet." After about a year of asking, I went into the office, sat down with Bob, and asked, "Can I open Syracuse?" His answer both surprised and delighted me. He said, "Yes, we are ready. Go open the market!" I was so excited as I left his office—until it hit me that I would actually have to open the market. Then a sinking feeling came over me, like "Oh, crap! What have I gotten myself into?" Now I had to perform.

Opening the Market

It was November when I was told I could open the market. The first thing I did was drive to Syracuse and get a phonebook. In 1990, there were hardly any cell phones, let alone smartphones. Phonebooks were a salesperson's best friend. I decided I would start the week after the new year because that's when everyone was ready to make a change.

During the December holidays, I scoured the phonebook for any leads I could find and wrote them on my notepad. I must have had more than one hundred suspects.

Huff's support was critical in this. They committed to the Syracuse market 100 percent, and they knew it was going to take time to develop. They understood that there would be weeks when little or no product would be on the truck, and they would have to deliver no matter what. I set a timeline of six weeks until we shipped the first truck.

I spent the week after the new year in my office making cold-call phone appointments, weeding out the prospects from the suspects, and ranking them based on their interest level and potential. The list dwindled fast to about twenty-five solid prospects.

I made my first calls into the market, introduced the company, gave out credit applications, and got lists of items to quote. What I discovered is that I had two main competitors. One delivered every other week, but the dominant competitor competed directly with the distributors they serviced. Huff offered weekly delivery and the promise not to compete with our customers. It was a compelling unique selling proposition, and the customers were eager to support our efforts.

The Moment of Truth

After about two months of delivering, we were in a cycle of getting a good week and then a light week. It went this way for a while, until one week we had just two skids on the truck. The warehouse manager called me and was rightly concerned. I understood his concerns, but I also knew the territory was building and that this was a temporary issue. I convinced him to ship the truck and that things would be better moving forward. He did, and that was the turning point. We didn't have a week like that again. Within six months we knew the territory would be a success, and in one year the territory was viable, growing, and making money. The key to success was the commitment made by Huff and the faith they had in my ability to deliver sales. It was truly a team effort.

That Will Never Happen Again

One part of my job with Huff was conducting sales meetings. I was always very good one-on-one, but standing in front of a crowd was a different thing. I was scheduled to do a sales meeting for a customer, but never having done one, I was completely unprepared—and I had never spoken before a group. I can't properly express how badly the meeting went. I left completely embarrassed and said to myself, "That will never happen again." A few months later, I saw an advertisement in the paper for a Dale Carnegie class on public speaking. It was very expensive, so I asked Phil if the company would pay for me to attend. Without much hesitation he said yes. I was excited to learn how to speak in public. The classes changed my life. In twelve weeks, I went from the world's worst speaker to a pretty decent speaker. At least, I was comfortable speaking to groups. The course also taught me how important preparation is to my confidence. In speaking, as in life, the more prepared you are, the more confident you will be. If you have a fear of public speaking, I highly recommend taking a Dale Carnegie course. It will increase your level of success and quality of life dramatically.

CHAPTER 11

You Are Who You Sell

A salesperson is a direct reflection
of the customers they serve.
—Michael Mirarchi

Through the years, I have had reps ride with me and visit my accounts. They all say the same thing. It goes something like, "Man, your customers are all really great people." I always respond that I don't sell to customers who aren't great. I never have and never will. My customers are all great. I genuinely like and respect them, and we have excellent relationships. I work with only the best customers, and this formula has been successful for me for a long time. I can tell you everything about a salesperson without meeting him or her. I only need to meet the salesperson's customers, and I can tell you not only the individual's point of view but also a lot about him or her as a person.

If you are having trouble gaining quality customers, you simply need to look in the mirror to understand why you are attracting the customers you are. We naturally attract people in our lives who mirror ourselves. If you improve yourself, you will naturally attract better customers.

Are you having problems with your customers focusing mainly on price? The real question is, are you selling on price alone?

Are your customers disrespectful of your time? The real question is, do you value what you bring to the table as a salesperson?

Do your customers always have complaints? The real question is, do you complain about your company and circumstances?

Are your customers running you ragged with unreasonable demands? The real question is, are you subservient to your customers?

Are your customers struggling to stay in business? The real question is, are you a product pusher, or are you focused on customer success?

Do the majority of your customers have trouble paying their bills? The real question is, how are your finances?

Do you have trouble negotiating good agreements? The real question is, are you too needy?

Do you have customers who are angry and disrespectful? The real question is, do you respect yourself?

Do you have issues with your margins? The real question is, are you selling products or solutions?

Are your prices always too high? The real question is, are you asking good questions?

Do your customers blame everyone else for their issues? The real question is, are you accountable and responsible?

The bottom line is that if you want to improve the quality of your business, customers, employees, or relationships, you will need to improve yourself.

The real question is, are you willing to make the investment?

CHAPTER 12

THE TOP TEN TRAITS OF A SUCCESSFUL SALESPERSON

The only place success comes before work is in the dictionary.
—VINCE LOMBARDI

If you are just starting your sales career or you want to become better, it's important to know the traits of the most successful salespeople. The goal of any salesperson is to *create a favorable atmosphere that leads to a sale.* The following ten traits will help you to become a top performer.

10. Be yourself.

The biggest lesson I learned from my first mentor was that I couldn't sell like him. When I read books and went to training early in my career, I was often frustrated that I couldn't sell like an expert. I would try, but after a while I would go back to what worked for me. Then I realized that if I could incorporate just one or two things that I learned, it would be effective, and it helped me. The key is to be yourself and sell the way that works best for you.

9. Be curious.

Successful salespeople are genuinely curious about their customers and how to help them. They ask a lot of questions and understand the customer's needs before offering a solution. They listen much more than they talk. Business owner and trainer Bill Allen said, "The more interested you are, the more interesting you will be." If you are focused on the customer and his or her needs, you will be ahead of the pack.

8. Be present.

Today's salesperson is required to be a masterful multitasker. When top salespeople are with a customer, they are fully present and completely focused on the meeting. They have the ability to compartmentalize and keep the customer as their focus. These salespeople aren't looking at their phones or, worse yet, taking phone calls during a meeting. If this sounds like you, turn off your cell phone or leave it in your car before making a sales call.

7. Be consistent.

Top salespeople do what they say and say what they do consistently. They can be counted on to follow through, return phone calls promptly, and show up to meetings on time. The bottom line is that they are reliable.

6. Be likable.

Top salespeople embrace their roles. They act, dress, and present themselves in a professional manor. They don't do anything to create a negative impression, such as wearing strong perfume or cologne, showing bling, exposing tattoos, and the like. You never know what will turn off a customer, and the most successful salespeople do everything they can to create a positive impression. They are likable and fun to be around.

5. Be positive.

We all have personal problems, trials, and issues. Top salespeople keep their problems to themselves; they do not share them with their customers. No matter how much it seems that your customers are interested in your problems, they are not. No matter how badly your day is going, don't bog down your customer with your troubles. They have problems of their own and your goal is to brighten their day, not make it worse.

4. Be respectful.

Top salespeople are always respectful of their customers' time. They make appointments, arrive promptly for them, and end meetings when they are over. They never overstay their welcome. Never assume that a customer has time to talk with you or engage you in a meeting unless you ask for permission.

3. Be persistent.

Persistence is a trait of all top salespeople. They have the ability to accept rejection and not take it personally while continuing to move toward their goals. It's one thing to have goals, but it's another to relentlessly pursue them. Top salespeople are tenacious about pursuing top customers and their goals.

2. Be an owner.

The most successful people in any business take ownership of their positions and work and act like they own the company. They make decisions and spend money like an owner. They think, and act, like they own the company.

1. Be honest.

Top salespeople act with integrity. They never overpromise and always overdeliver. The premise that you have to be dishonest in any way to be a top salesperson is completely false. If you are liked and trusted by your customers, then you are well on your way to becoming a top performer.

CHAPTER 13

The ABCs of Sales Growth: How to Increase Sales by 30 Percent

If you create space, it will be filled with something.
—Anonymous

Growing 30 percent in one year is a nice accomplishment. Growing 30 percent a year for fifteen straight years with two separate companies is something completely different. One principle I learned is that you can't put water into a full glass. You must keep emptying your glass so that you can keep filling it. About every six months my workweek fills up, and I reevaluate how I spend my time. In other words, I create space. I either reconfigure my territory routes or my schedule, or I evaluate my customers. Each time I do it, my productivity increases dramatically. It's a natural law that a space created will be filled with something. It's the law of vacuum. The key is filling the space with something productive.

Here is a simple way to manage your customers and spend your time where it will be most effective. The following exercise will take about thirty minutes and increase your time capacity by 20 to 30 percent.

Ranking Your Customers

Take your customer list and rank it using four criteria:

1. Volume
2. Margin
3. Pay
4. PITA

Volume. Each company is different, and only you will know the numbers that make sense. If your customer is over your set number for a good volume customer, he or she gets one point.

Margin. If your customer hits the threshold you set for a good margin, he or she gets one point. Everything you do is for nothing if you can't make a profit. You can be the best company in the world, but if you are out of business, your customers lose. There is nothing wrong with a fair profit. It is why business is done.

Pay. This is the most critical item. If your customer pays within terms, he or she gets one point (I give an extra five days). If they pay thirty or more days late, subtract one point. If they pay sixty days late, subtract two points. Most salespeople who get an order think they have done something. They don't realize that at the point of taking an order the only thing you got is a *loan.* There is no order until the bill is paid. The salespeople who believe that credit is not the responsibility of sales are flat wrong. It is your responsibility as a salesperson to sell to customers who won't put your company at risk. You should get involved if collecting money becomes an issue. You are part of a team and that includes the credit department.

PITA. If you haven't figured it out yet, PITA means "pain in the a**!" These are the customers who drive you mad. They continually have issues with your product or service, and of course your price is never low enough. As you would expect, they are notoriously slow payers, so they take up an extraordinary amount of your time and generally aren't appreciative of the value you bring to the table. If they are *not* a PITA, they get one point.

Now add up the points. Use the following scale to rank your customers:

Four points = A customer
Three points = B customer
Two points = C customer
One point = D customer
Zero points = "Are you kidding?" customer

A customers. These are your best customers. They love to deal with you, and they are a pleasure to deal with. These customers are true partners and should be treated as such.

B customers. These customers are the backbone of your company. They are good, solid customers on whom you can build your business.

C customers. You need to use caution when dealing with these customers. Why are they C customers? It is up to you to either raise them up to an A or a B customer, or weed them out.

D customers. These are the donkey customers you can't afford to spend much time with and should consider firing.

"Are you kidding?" customers. I am always amazed by how much time is wasted on these customers. Do yourself a favor and fire them. Think about it: if you get rid of them, they will have to buy product from someone. It might as well be your competition! Let your competitors deal with them while you focus on picking up their A customers.

Using the 80/20 Rule

Most salespeople spend 80 percent of their time on 80 percent of their customers, who make up 20 percent of their business. Why? Because those customers demand much more service. What if you reverse that and spend 80 percent of your time on the top 20 percent of your customers who do 80 percent of your business?

If after ranking your customers you find that you are spending too much time on the C, D, and "Are you kidding?" customers, weed them out. This way you will pick up one or two days of free time that you can spend on your best customers, as well as prospecting for more, which is the key to massive growth. It is using the law of vacuum to your benefit. If you do this on a regular basis, you will enjoy sales increases and your life will be much better.

CHAPTER 14

Increase Sales by Being an Apple Picker

All apples taste the same no matter where on the tree they were picked.
—Michael Mirarchi

An apple orchard owner was in a real jam. She had only two apple pickers for the beginning of the harvest because the rest couldn't make it to the farm on time. She looked for other help, but none could be found. She called her two pickers into her office and told them, "Look, we are in a real jam here. Go out and pick as many apples as you can until we can get more workers, which will be in at least three days."

So picker number one went out to the first tree and started picking apples. He was a very good worker and picked every single apple off each tree until it was bare.

As he was high on the ladder, he noticed apple picker number two going from tree to tree in what looked like a disorganized manner. He was picking all of the apples he could reach from the bottom of the trees. "What a fool!" thought apple picker number one. He is leaving all of those apples on the trees. Apple picker number one thought for sure he would beat picker number two by far.

At the end of the third day, the owner called in the apple pickers and told them help had finally arrived. She appreciated all they had done, and she was going to pay them double for the apples they picked.

Apple picker number one was very happy to hear this because he knew he did an excellent job picking every apple off the trees. He picked sixty bushels of apples and collected his pay. His jaw then hit the ground in disbelief when we saw that apple picker number two had picked three times more apples—a whopping 180 bushels!

Apple picker number one was furious and let the orchard owner know what had happened.

He said, "I picked every apple off the trees just like you said, while apple picker number two simply went from tree to tree, picking everything he could grab."

She said, "I get the same amount of money for apples picked from the top or the bottom of the tree. It makes no difference to me or my buyers where the apples came from, as long as they are ripe and delicious to eat."

As a salesperson, are you apple picker number one, wasting time high up in the tree, or apple picker number two, who collected as many apples within reach as he could as fast as he could?

It doesn't matter how long it took or how hard it was to get sales, because at the end of the day, sales dollars are all the same. As a salesperson, you must make every minute count. Calling on unproductive accounts is like picking apples from the top of the tree. Your time is better spent picking the low-hanging fruit. One sales call is one sales call. That call can lead to $10 in sales or $10,000 in sales, because it is essentially the same call and process. The key is understanding where your greatest potential for sales lies at any given time and working on that, even if you have to skip over another customer or deal to get there. You can only be in one place at a time. Make sure the time you are investing is productive, and the sales increases will follow.

CHAPTER 15

EFF THE ECONOMY

Excuses change nothing, but make everyone feel better.
—MASON COOLEY

The years since the 2008 recession have been challenging economically, leading to phrases like "flat is the new up," which I believe is garbage. The fact is that everything is either growing or dying. Flat is down no matter how you look at it.

The only way you can blame the economy for your woes is if you have more than 80 percent market share.

My question is, what is your market share within a ten-mile radius of your building? What is your market share in your territory? Most times the answer to that question is a very low number, less than 10 percent.

If you have only a 10 percent market share, how can you blame the economy? I say eff the economy! The economy is an excuse for you not to grow. How about replacing "flat is the new up" with "10 percent growth is the new up," and let that be your new reality.

CHAPTER 16

EFF THE COMPETITION

If you look out the side window while driving, you will crash the car.
—ANONYMOUS

A new competitor enters your market. How do you react? Do you change your strategy or keep doing what got you where you are?

Although it is wise to be aware of what your competition is doing, it is just as wise not to be too focused on them and to focus instead on striving for excellence. If you strive for excellence, you won't have to worry about the competition.

Consider this. A new competitor offering five-dollar haircuts opened across the street from an established hair salon. The established salon had two choices: lower its prices or focus on excellence.

If the established salon had lowered its prices, its image and ultimately its business would have suffered.

Instead, the salon hung a large banner out front that read, "We fix $5 haircuts!" Their business increased by 20 percent, and not long afterward, the competitor went out of business.

Sometimes we get so focused on the competition that we lose sight of what we must do to achieve excellence.

The companies that are swamped by the competition are the companies that are not changing and innovating.

If you are continually striving for excellence, innovating, and moving your business forward, your competition will be the one up all night worrying about you.

CHAPTER 17

THE FORMULA FOR SELLING PROFITABLY

If your conduct is determined solely by considerations of profit you will arouse great resentment.
—CONFUCIUS

In this age of unlimited information, Internet retailers, and increased competition, is it possible to maintain and grow margins? The simple answer is *yes*. I hear many conversations that refer to "the race to zero" or "flat is the new up." To accept these statements is to admit defeat. Once you believe it is possible to increase sales and margins in this age, you will be on your way. The following formula will help you make it happen:

Creativity × Confidence + Fit = Profitability

The Formula for Selling Profitably

I was challenged to come up with a presentation on this topic a few years ago, and it got me thinking: What is a profitable sale? As I thought about my most profitable sales, this formula came to mind: C × C + F = P, or Creativity × Confidence + Fit = Profitability. All profitable sales have these three elements at some stage of the sales process.

Creativity. There were many times when I was faced with having to lower margins, and I was able to come up with a creative solution that preserved and even enhanced the margins. The customer was the winner because I was able to offer a solution that allowed the customer to get a better product and save money. Here is the rub: these solutions must be sold. The profitably of an item is in direct proportion to how well it uniquely solves a problem. To expect to make money when five other companies are trying to sell the same solution is not realistic and will result in lower margins. If your competition is selling commodity products, then you must offer value-added solutions that will work better and save the customer money. Knowing the difference between the price and the cost is the key to selling the best solution to your customer, allowing you to make the biggest profits. You must have a salmon mentality and consistently swim against the tide.

Confidence. Have you been in a situation where you were being sold something and you asked a question that completely threw off the salesperson? What happened is that the salesperson wasn't prepared for the question and lost confidence. You pick up on it immediately, and the sale doesn't happen. Why? Because you as a buyer lose confidence that you will get the right solution for your needs. Creativity is great, but without confidence the sale doesn't happen.

The reasons for a loss of confidence vary. Lack of training and practice are two of the biggest reasons. Role-playing should be an essential part of your training; it helps sales reps have confidence when unexpected situations and questions arise. Another reason for a lack of confidence is the lack of good information. What does your price book look like? Are the descriptions clear? Do your reps have all of the information they need to answer product questions with confidence?

Fit. You can have the most creative approach and an abundance of confidence, but if the solution doesn't make sense, then the sale is lost. To get the right fit, you must do your homework. Preparation and information gathering (asking questions) are the keys to a proper fit.

There are two types of sales calls. *Sales call one* is having the goal to get the sale. If your purpose is simply to get the sale, you will likely be unsuccessful; if you are successful, the sale won't be as profitable. In addition, the customer will most likely get buyer's remorse because the fit wasn't right.

Sales call two is to help your customer be more successful. It is a completely different call. To help the customer be successful, you must understand his or her needs and objectives so that you can offer the best solution and ultimately help the customer to achieve his or her goals.

If you take a creative approach, have confidence, and offer solutions that fit the customer's needs, the price becomes less important, and you become a trusted advisor instead of an order taker.

Selling China Creatively

When I was selling restaurant equipment and supplies, I called on a customer who was looking to replace her china. She asked for a quote, which I gave to her, and she asked me to come back the following week for the order. I stopped back the next week, and when I asked about the china, she said that Sysco beat my price. I asked for the price that they quoted and then proceeded to beat Sysco's price. She gave me the order. It turned out that it was a special order for Sysco, so they had china in their warehouse for a long time.

Occasionally I would rub it in to the Sysco rep when I saw him. The problem was that because I had to go so low on the price, I didn't make any money. A month or so later, another company down the street was looking to replace its china. Their issue was breakage, and they were looking for a solution to solve the problem. In our sales meeting, Corning introduced a new china called Comcor. You may know the product on the retail side as Corelle. The china was actually made of glass and resisted breakage. The best part was that Sysco didn't carry the product. I got a sample plate and brought it on my next call to the account. I walked into the kitchen with the sample plate and tossed it into the air. The look on the workers' faces was one of shock as they all waited for the plate to shatter into a million pieces. The plate hit the ground—and nothing happened. Everyone was amazed that it didn't break. Not only did I make the sale, but I made it at full price. To this day, the company says it was the best purchase it ever made. This story embodies the formula for selling profitably. I took a creative approach with full confidence that the product would perform, knowing that it was a perfect fit. The result was a profitable sale.

CHAPTER 18

Winning by Changing the Playing Field

Creativity is putting your imagination to work, and it's produced the most extraordinary results in human culture.
—Ken Robinson

When I was a teenager, a new Carvel Ice Cream Shop opened in our town. For years, our town was dominated by Dairy Queen, so to build some buzz, Carvel decided to hold an ice-cream-eating contest. I was excited to participate along with about twenty others.

While describing the rules, they also announced the prizes. The top prize went to the person who finished eating his or her dish of ice cream first, and other prizes were announced for other categories, including the messiest face.

As soon as the prizes were announced, I immediately thought, "There is no way I'm going to win the eating contest, so I'm going for the messiest face award." Then I thought, "I hope no one else thinks of it."

The moment the judge said go, I smashed my face into the plate of ice cream and smeared it around. I don't think I ate one bite.

After picking my face up out of the ice cream, it was obvious I would get the award because no one else had had the same idea. While nineteen people were competing for the same prize, I won my award in the first five seconds.

I received my reward and enjoyed free ice cream all summer. It was a great prize and a good example of winning by taking a creative approach.

Many times the victory is won for those who have a salmon mentality and travel away from the crowd. The key to success is to look at what people are doing today and then go in the opposite direction.

Profits are made in the places where competition doesn't exist. It's up to us to discover those places and dominate the space. Then, when the competition catches on, you will be onto the next area, always a step ahead.

CHAPTER 19

THE THEORY OF SCATTERING MICE

There is nothing less attractive than neediness.
—MICHAEL MIRARCHI

When I was in high school, an interesting thing happened the moment I started dating a girl. All of a sudden, there were two or three other girls who wanted to date me. I became very attractive and desirable. It seemed like I could date just about any girl in the school, and my confidence soared. Then the day came when we broke up. I was suddenly available, but then the other girls were nowhere to be found. They scattered like mice and left me wondering what happened.

The Hockey Game

I never thought much about it until years later when I took several kids to a hockey game. I had three extra tickets and wanted to sell them. A guy came up to me and wanted to buy two tickets. It was early, and I had plenty of time to sell the tickets, so I held out. I wanted to sell all three tickets, not two. The guy came back again asking for two tickets, and I was comfortable saying no. Game time was now approaching, and he came back a third time. I really wanted to sell all three tickets, and so I continued to delay—and then it happened. The buyer changed his mind and started walking away. All of a sudden, I became very needy, chased him down, and sold the two tickets to him at less than the original price

I was asking. Afterward, I realized what had happened. It was the theory of scattering mice. The needier you are, the less attractive you become. The theory applies in sales, negotiations, dating, finding a job, and in just about every area of your life. If you watch *Shark Tank* or *Pawn Stars*, you will see the theory of scattering mice in action constantly.

Wants and Needs

One difference between very successful people and others is that very successful people *want* things, and less successful people *need* things. When successful people want something, they will take the emotion out of the decision as much as possible and get the best deal. They won't date the first person to come along or take the first job offer or deal. These people are the most attractive. Being needy not only makes you less attractive but also leads to poor decisions. I see it in sales all the time. Needy people will deal with customers who dump all over them because they need the numbers, and the customers take advantage of it. Do yourself a favor and fire that customer immediately. You don't need customers who suck the life out of you and make you miserable—no matter how large they are. I can guarantee that you are most likely losing money on them anyway.

Job Hunting Tip

When looking for a job, please don't post it as the title on your résumé or LinkedIn profile. Which do you think is more attractive: Jane Smith (Currently Looking for Employment) or Jane Smith (President) of J. Smith Enterprises? You are far better off starting a company of any type than stating that you are out of work. I read articles all the time about how it is much harder to find a job when you are out of work. You are setting yourself up to be a victim of the theory of scattering mice, and you will automatically have a persona that is much less attractive. The bonus is that if you start a business, it just might take off, and you won't need to find another job!

Awareness is the first step to moving away from being needy. Understanding the theory of scattering mice will help you to have better relationships, become a better negotiator, gain more sales, get a better job, and be a more attractive person.

CHAPTER 20

WHY YOUR PRICE MATTERS

Nowadays people know the price of everything
and the value of nothing.
—LORD HENRY WOTTON

During our recent move when we were cleaning out our house, we found an old TV that we didn't need any longer. We decided to donate it to Goodwill. When the truck came to pick it up, along with the other items we were donating, the workers told us that they wouldn't take the TV because "digital TVs are so cheap that no one wants the analog models any longer."

"We can't give them away," said one of the other workers.

Then, our nephew told us a story about one of his friends who wanted to get rid of his analog TV. He put it out on the curb with a sign that read "Free." After getting no takers, he decided to change the sign to read "For Sale $50." A few hours later, he walked outside, and the TV was gone. Someone had stolen it!

As we laughed about the story, the lesson was clear: *the way we price our products and services has a direct effect on the perception of their value in the customer's mind.*

If your sales are lagging, you may need to reevaluate the price you are charging. If your price is too low, you may be creating a negative perception of the quality of your products or service.

Early in my career on a sales call to a nursing home, the buyer asked if I had a cleaning chemical they were using. Although I didn't have the brand they were using, I had one that was comparable. When the buyer asked about the price, I quoted the lowest price I had. It turned out that the buyer was paying a much higher price than I quoted, and she said, "It can't be the same item because it's too cheap." Even though I tried to convince her otherwise, it was too late. The damage had been done, and I didn't get the sale. A comparable example is when you are shopping for something and you look at three different brands. They all look similar, with maybe a few feature differences. As you try to make a decision about which one to buy, you look at the prices. Often in this scenario, you will pick the item priced in the middle. You are concerned that the lower-priced item is too cheap and won't hold up, and you don't want the most expensive, so you choose the middle one. All of the items could be exactly the same, but the middle-priced item seems like the most practical choice.

The bottom line is that the price you charge matters. Try changing your prices, even on a small scale, and see what happens.

CHAPTER 21

The Question to Help You Slay the Price Objection Dragon

I never learn anything talking. I only learn things when I ask questions.
—Lou Holtz

As salespeople, the top objection we hear about is price. Many times buyers throw the price objection at us because it's an easy way to get rid of the seller.

When you get a price objection, it's important to understand whether price is the real objection or if there is another reason why the buyer doesn't want to move forward. If you can get the buyer to open up and tell you the actual reason he or she does not want to buy, you will be able to address it, thus increasing your chances of making the sale.

When a customer objects to your price, make sure you are quoting against an equivalent product or service. Once that is determined, ask the following question: Other than the price, is there any other reason why you won't buy? When you ask this question you will most likely understand the real reason why the customer is objecting. Once you address the main objection(s), you may find that the price isn't as much of an issue as you think.

The key to success in sales is gaining the correct knowledge and insight about the buyer's needs, wants, and desires and then matching them with the proper product or solution that will allow the buyer to be successful. At that point you won't be selling anything; the buyers will be selling to themselves.

CHAPTER 22

COLD-CALLING SUCCESS

When you do what you fear most, then you can do anything.
—STEPHEN RICHARDS

Today, many people say that cold calling is dead. I believe that cold calling continues to be an effective way to gain new customers. Cold calling can be done over the phone, by e-mail, or by physically going to the location. There are now services that offer to generate leads for your team by cold calling and developing relationships and then handing the warm leads over to your team. They are very effective. If you are not using a service, the goal of a cold call in the B2B world is to gather information with the possibility of getting an appointment. Expecting to see or spend time with someone is unrealistic. If you can get the name of the correct contact person, his or her contact information, and the best time to reach the individual, then the cold call is a success. If you can get an appointment, it's a bonus. Respect of time is the key.

The story I told about getting my first customer with Huff is an extremely unusual circumstance. If that happened today, knowing what I know now, I would be very skeptical about a customer who places an order on the first call. It is most likely a credit issue or some other problem. If you make a cold call and expect to see someone, you are asking for trouble. You will quickly become an annoyance and lose any opportunity to make the sale. A simple inquiry about whether the customer is a potential fit, asking about the person in charge, getting his or her contact information, and learning the best time to contact the individual is sufficient. After you make the first contact, a follow-up call or e-mail to set up an appointment is appropriate. Then you have given the proper respect and will be able to have a fruitful sales call. The information-gathering phase, including cold calls, is essential to sales success. There is so much information available online today about your prospective client that you can know almost everything about a potential customer. Researching your prospects will tell them that you are interested in their companies and are serious about doing business with them. The quest to continue to develop new prospects is ongoing.

I have found that LinkedIn is one of the best tools through which to contact new prospects. I have gotten in touch with company CEOs just by connecting with them and sending them InMail. As with any other tool, you must be active on LinkedIn and contribute value to the community. The bottom line is that you must always be actively cold-calling and drumming up new prospects. After securing information from a cold call, immediately connect with the customer on LinkedIn. It is another touch and a way to establish credibility with the prospect.

You have to expect to lose 5–10 percent of your business each year for various reasons. Your book of business must continue to be replenished in order to keep growing. Cold calling is a vital tool and must be used consistently.

CHAPTER 23

Why Do You Make Sales Calls?

Do right. Do your best. Treat others as you want to be treated.
—Lou Holtz

"Why do you make sales calls?" When I ask salespeople this question during sales training, I receive the following most common answers:

1. To make money
2. To make the sale
3. To support my family

All of these answers have one thing in common: they are centered in the salesperson's world, not in the customer's.

Having a Purpose

When selling, it's important to have a purpose, which is centered in the customer's world. If you are trying to make sales with a purpose centered in your world, your presentation and approach will be focused on your desire to get the order. This will be apparent to the buyer and result in immediate resistance.

A purpose centered in your customer's world is a completely different sales call and process. It will allow you to properly prepare for the sales call and be interested in your customer's goals, needs, and desires. Ask good questions and offer them solutions that best meet their needs.

As I was driving down the highway, I saw a truck that had a company mission printed on the side. It said, "Success Through Customer Satisfaction." Even though that sounds nice, it is a mission that is centered in the company's world. What if it said, "Satisfaction Through Customer Success"? The meaning is completely changed. Customer satisfaction alone isn't good enough. Many customers have been satisfied right out of business. We must be focused on our customers' successes and do everything in our power to help them achieve their goals.

The bottom line is that if you want to increase sales, you must help your customers get what they want. If you make the shift to help your customers become more successful, your sales increase and your customers will be more loyal because they will view you as a trusted advisor and not just another person trying to get their business.

CHAPTER 24

Mr. Bubble: The Best Example of Overpromising Ever!

Politicians are the same all over. They promise to build bridges even when there are no rivers.
—Nikita Khrushchev

When I was about seven or eight years old, I pestered my parents for weeks to get a box of Mr. Bubble bubble bath. Finally, they broke down and bought it for me.

I couldn't wait for bath time. I was so excited to see Mr. Bubble and all of the bubbles that would float all over the bathroom. It would be a party; after all, it was on the commercials.

My mom filled the tub and sprinkled in the Mr. Bubble. And then—nothing happened. It was just a bubble bath. No Mr. Bubble, no bubbles floating all over the bathroom, no singing, just a plain old bubble bath. It was one of the biggest disappointments in my young life.

After I got married I shared the story with my wife, and what do you know—she had the same experience!

Overpromising always ends badly for the same reason that I was so disappointed about Mr. Bubble. The expectations you set when selling to a customer matter. It's always better to underpromise and overdeliver. If the customers' expectations are in check, you can easily exceed them. If expectations are set too high, the customer will most likely end up disappointed. When that happens, it's almost impossible to recover and build a long-lasting relationship.

CHAPTER 25

CLOSING THE SALE

There is no magic or secret to closing a sale
—MICHAEL MIRARCHI

Throughout my career I opened hundreds of new accounts and businesses, and I always felt inferior that I didn't have a magic closing line or phrase to get the sale.

I kept hearing about asking early and often and about all these cool closing lines that just felt awkward to me. I had no trouble getting business, but I never used pressure or fancy lines to do it.

In fact, I wrote this chapter last because initially I wasn't planning to include it. Then I thought, "What sales book doesn't have a chapter on closing the sale?"

How did I close all of the business I conducted over thirty years? The answer is that there is no secret.

I simply followed the principles outlined in this book and the customers closed the sale themselves. There are different types of selling, and sometimes you have only one chance to face the buyer, and that requires a different approach. The wholesale distribution business is one where relationship building is the key to success, which is why my approach works so well.

Most good buyers are wise to fancy closing lines, and it just makes them angry when you try to use them. It's important to ask for the order but only in a respectful way that's natural and honest.

Throughout my career, my customers have had no buyer's remorse because they knew what they were buying, and they got what they were promised.

Many businesses offer good quality products at a competitive price. What differentiates you? There must be a good reason for a buyer to switch from their current supplier. Your goal in making a sales call is to discover how you can be a benefit to the buyer and their company. If the buyer sees no benefit for them they aren't going to switch no matter how hard you try.

The key to sales success is that it has to be a team effort. You could be the best salesperson in the world, but if your company or your team drops the ball, you'll be unsuccessful. Great salespeople get just one or two extra chances—that's it.

The bottom line is that the entire team has to perform for any salesperson to be successful.

When your team is behind you, your confidence level will be high, because you know deep in your heart that your company will deliver. It makes all the difference and will make closing much easier.

Do yourself a favor and thank your team often; show your appreciation for their efforts. If not for them, you would be dead in the water.

CHAPTER 26

DEFENDING YOUR TERRITORY

It's just as important to defend what you have built as it is to gain new business.
—MICHAEL MIRARCHI

Once you establish yourself as a top salesperson, you'll realize that there aren't that many other good reps who are your competition. There just aren't a lot of top salespeople, period.

What happens when your competition hires a good salesperson in your territory and they start taking your business? When new reps are hired, there is often an initial sales surge, which fades away over time.

One time a new rep was hired in my territory, and after the initial surge, a funny thing happened: I kept hearing her name. She persisted until she started gaining some business and making inroads. The reality is that top salespeople are going to get their share of business no matter how good you are. I was rightly concerned about the market share she was gaining, and I tried to figure out a way to defend my turf.

A few weeks later, I read an article about how a person moved up the corporate ladder by having her direct boss recruited away from the company. She had done this successfully many times and was promoted each time her boss was gone.

I called a recruiter in my industry and told him about this young salesperson and what a great candidate she would be for his firm. I sent him her contact information, and six months later she was hired away from my competition.

I was then able to regain the business I had lost, and since then the competitor hasn't hired a rep of that quality.

The reality is that there aren't that many top salespeople, so the chances that another one would be hired were slim to none. I've only had to use this tactic one time in my thirty years of selling, but that one time gained me millions of dollars of business.

CHAPTER 27

EIGHT SIGNALS YOU SHOULD WALK AWAY FROM A NEW PROSPECT

Bend over backward for your customers, never bow down.
—SAM SKODACEK

As discussed in previous chapters, new accounts are the key to a growing and thriving business. Salespeople are always under pressure to bring in new business and, because of the pressure, too many become needy and ignore the warning signals that a prospect will likely become a difficult customer. The following are eight signals that, if present, should cause you to pause before taking an order.

1. The prospect isn't respectful of your time or team.

I made an appointment with a prospect for 3:00 p.m. I was fifteen minutes early for the appointment. I sat and waited past 3:15, approaching 3:30. At precisely 3:30, I got up and told the receptionist that I was leaving because I had another appointment. As I was walking out the door, the prospect came running after me and apologized. We then sat down and had a good, though shorter, meeting, and the prospect became a great customer. My father-in-law had a saying: "Bend over backward for your customers, but never bow down." In this case, if I hadn't set the tone, then the customer wouldn't have had the proper respect for my time. A salesperson should never be subservient to a prospect or a client; otherwise, your customer will disrespect you and your company.

2. The prospect becomes agitated when discussing credit terms.

One hard-and-fast rule I have is to discuss payment terms early in the sales process. This is never an issue unless, of course, the customer has a problem paying his or her bills. Two things happen: the customer discloses to you that he or she pays late, or gets irritated. Both are big warning flags that you shouldn't do business with the prospect. Many salespeople don't understand that a sale isn't made until the bill is paid. Otherwise it is only a loan.

3. The prospect is very demanding.

I once had a prospective customer call to ask for prices on a line we stocked. I sent the customer a credit application and let him know that I would be happy to send him a price list once the credit application was processed. He then called customer service and rudely demanded pricing and samples. The moment I heard about it, I called and told him that we didn't want to do business with his company. He was obviously upset. A few years later, his company went out of business and stuck my competition for $100,000. Never tolerate a prospect or a customer who isn't respectful to you or your employees; it is unprofessional and unacceptable.

4. The prospect is too eager to do business.

If someone calls you to do business, the first questions you should ask are "How did you hear about our company?" and "Why are you calling?" The answers are very important because many times when customers are in trouble, they will try to get new vendors to extend credit terms. It never ends well and is not worth your time and trouble.

5. Something doesn't feel right about the transaction.

Sometimes everything is going well and you get a sinking feeling about the transaction. It is important not to ignore these feelings. You might not walk away, but more investigation is needed before moving forward.

6. The prospect sets an unreasonable deadline.

Early in my career, I called on a prospect who was looking to buy special-order china. He needed it in six weeks for his restaurant opening. I went to our buyer and asked him if we could meet the deadline. He said it would be very tight, but we should be able to do it. For a new rep, that was a green light, so I assured the customer that he would have his china. Well, it didn't come in on time, so the customer canceled the order and never bought from my company again. I found out later that the customer had come to us only after his other suppliers said they couldn't meet the deadline. You're always better off underpromising and not getting the order than overpromising and losing the prospect forever.

7. The prospect is only focused on the cost of goods.

I called on a large account once, and after the first meeting, the customer liked what we had to offer and asked me to come back the next week to get an order. I arrived on time, and the customer pulled out a spreadsheet, asking the price on every item and ordering it only if we had the lowest price. Even though I got a nice order, I asked the customer if this is what I should expect each week. When he said yes, I told him that I would be happy to ship the current order, but I wouldn't be returning after that. Our company has much more to offer than just selling on price. While my competition is lined up waiting to get "spreadsheeted" by this customer and others, I focus on the prospects who value what we bring to the table.

8. There isn't a good match between your offerings and your prospect's needs.

I have gained hundreds of customers throughout my career, and occasionally it just seemed that everything was wrong. You sell brand X, and they buy brand Y. You deliver on Wednesday, and they need it on Thursday. Your minimum order is X, and it is too high. They need a certain product, and it is not in stock. It seems everything goes wrong. When this happens, it is a big sign that you don't mesh with the customer.

In most of these cases, it is better to move on than to force a sale. Most often, these customers don't become "A" customers and frequently turn out to be difficult, which results in wasted time and money and even a tarnished reputation.

Remember, you don't have to sell to every prospect. There are plenty who will mesh with you and your company. If you focus on them, your sales will increase dramatically and your life will be much easier.

CHAPTER 28

THE HISTORY OF TOILET PAPER: THE TALE OF THE SHRINKING ROLL

Price is what you pay. Value is what you get.
—WARREN BUFFETT

Because I sell toilet paper for a living, I feel it's appropriate to share with you some insights into and challenges facing this industry. We all have gone to a grocery store to buy a product and notice that the package is smaller and that there is less product in the package. This is the history of toilet paper.

I have been in the commercial toilet-paper distribution business since 1985 and have seen many changes. One of the most dramatic is what I call "The History of Toilet Paper." There was a time when one specification for toilet tissue was sold. It was a five-hundred-count, 4.5 × 4.5-size sheet, two-ply roll, ninety-six rolls to a case. Everyone sold the same spec, and it was very easy to compete. Then someone got a brilliant idea: a 4.5 × 4.0, two-ply, five-hundred-sheet, ninety-six-roll case. It was about 12 percent less paper at 10 percent less cost. As it started to gain ground, distributors tried to fight back by selling the value of a full case, which saved money. Slowly but surely, the market moved to the new full size until someone came up with another brilliant idea. If 4.5 × 4.0 worked, let's try 4.5 × 3.8. Then 4.5 × 3.8 became the norm, and even smaller sizes emerged.

Next came an eighty-count case instead of ninety-six, and the case and the roll kept shrinking. Most customers don't realize that they are getting less, and when they find out, many don't care. Consumers today have a price-per-package mentality. The larger issue is the amount of extra packaging it takes to make a smaller case and the amount of extra labor to change rolls. There is a huge difference between the price of the case and the cost a facility incurs by using cheaper rolls.

Jumbo-roll tissue was then developed and marketed as an alternative to single-roll tissue for large facilities, such as airports, schools, and sports stadiums. The biggest benefit was that because rolls were as large as four thousand feet, they would have to be changed less often and would save the customer labor costs. The largest selling of the jumbo-roll type is the nine-inch diameter roll, which contains one thousand feet of tissue. Someone got another brilliant idea and started selling an 850-foot roll, which then became 750 feet, then 600 feet, then 550 feet, then 500 feet, and now the footage has been removed and jumbo-roll tissue is being sold by pounds per case.

It all started with the shrinking coffee can. Several years ago, coffee makers started packing their coffee in twelve-ounce cans instead of one-pound cans. The media and some consumers were outraged. The coffee companies largely ignored the press, and when the change was ultimately accepted, other companies followed suit. They saw it as a way to increase prices without changing the cost per package. It is now commonplace for companies to shrink everything from cookies to diapers.

Paper Towels: Picking up less than ever. Paper Towels is another good example of the shrinking roll. One manufacturer was once ninety sheets per roll; then it went to eighty-four sheets, then seventy-two, then sixty-four, then fifty-two. Now a roll is forty sheets. That is less than half the size! You know the count has changed when you see "New and Improved" on the package. It should say, "Smaller than Before." This is not to say that improvements aren't made, but companies take full advantage of a product improvement to shrink the package when they want to raise the price.

How will this end? As long as customers keep accepting the smaller and lighter packages, this madness will continue. It is a race to zero that will end once the rolls get so small that customers reject them. Maybe it is time to go back to the 4.5 × 4.5 five-hundred-sheet roll of toilet tissue. We can call it a "New and Improved Double Roll" and get back to selling the benefits of buying a larger roll.

CHAPTER 29

The Key to Customer Loyalty

You don't earn loyalty in a day. You earn loyalty day-by-day.
—Jeffrey H. Gitomer

There is a belief today that customers are no longer loyal. Customers simply look for the best price with no regard for their current suppliers or the relationships they have built. Even though there are more choices to source product than ever before, and there are different players entering the market, the fact remains that price is not the biggest reason you are losing customers. I have been with Huff Paper for a long time, and I have customers who have been with us since the day I started. They are some of my best and most loyal ones even in this age of "no loyalty." Creating loyalty isn't based on just one factor. It is a combination of factors that creates a loyal customer. Excellent customer service, competitive pricing, and consistent follow-up all contribute.

Technology's Role

The onset of technology has dramatically changed how we communicate with our customers. Many times we call a company and get an automated answering service and, within moments, find ourselves pounding on the 0 key trying to get to a human. How can you expect loyalty if you aren't willing to engage your customers? We tend to overuse e-mail instead of picking up the phone and talking live with customers, especially when there is a problem to solve. Excellent service creates loyalty, and having person-to-person contact is still a big advantage.

The Bank Account

How do you gauge if you are in danger of losing a customer? If you have limited person-to-person contact, it is almost impossible to know.

In every relationship we keep score—consciously or not—including in our friendships and marriages and with our coworkers, employers, employees, and customers. Those who say they don't keep score are not being truthful. It is very important to be aware of these accounts so that you don't run a deficit.

The following is a good example of how this works. When our kids were younger, I used to go to a NASCAR race with my best friend for a weekend once a year. My wife had no issues with this and was, in fact, very supportive. On Friday when I left, we kissed and she wished me a good time. Of course, as soon as I left, the kids would get sick, and all heck would break loose. She wasn't the same person when I returned home on Sunday and rightfully so. Why? My bank account was drained. So I had to do things like send flowers, do dishes, cook, and take the kids to build my account back up. What do you think would happen if I got home on Sunday and told her I was going out drinking with the guys?

It's the same with your customers. Every business has missteps and mistakes. It's not the mistakes that matter but how you handle them. When there is a problem, your bank account will be down. If you don't respond to fix it to your customers' satisfaction, your account will be even lower. If you don't do anything substantial to rebuild your account, you will be in a deficit from which you may not be able to recover. The next thing you know, your competition will be taking your business and you will be wondering what happened.

To keep loyal customers, you must always be aware of your bank account, and you must work to keep your account balance up. Ensure that your company is customer friendly and that you keep person-to-person contact high. Showing that you truly care will make all the difference, and your customers will remain loyal well into the future.

CHAPTER 30

THE FIRST STEP TO A LOST CUSTOMER

When we take a customer's business for granted,
we are taking the first step out the door.
—MICHAEL MIRARCHI

At a conference, I was sitting with a customer who told me about a competitive salesperson with whom she was doing a large amount of business, but who seemed not to care about her business. She was frustrated because she liked dealing with the company and had for a long time, but she was feeling neglected.

I was very interested to understand this and as I probed deeper, she explained that she felt that because she had been such a good customer for so long, her salesperson was taking her for granted. When she asked for information, she wouldn't get a prompt reply; when she brought up a price objection, it wasn't addressed. The salesperson just didn't seem to care.

This was one of the easiest sales I ever made because all of the goodwill built up over the years was torn down by an unresponsive salesperson. Dissatisfaction and frustration took over, and the customer was ready to change.

When we take a customer's business for granted, we are taking the first step to losing that business. The funny thing is that it usually happens with our very best customers, because they are generally the easiest to service and complain very little.

Always take the time to thank your customers for their business and show them how much you appreciate their support.

CHAPTER 31

The Fastest Way to Lose a Sale

Perception is reality.
—Lee Atwater

Several years ago, my wife and I were shopping for furniture at Raymour and Flanigan. We were greeted by a salesperson whom we knew and had bought from before. As we walked around the store, we looked at a lamp and thought the price seemed high, which I noted to the salesperson. His response was amazing. He said, "Well, you know this is Paymore and Flanigan!" As we laughed, we were both taken aback by his comment. It was obviously an inside joke, but it seared an image into our minds to the point that I am including it in this book. We didn't buy there that day or since. Every time I see the company's commercials, drive by the store, or think about buying furniture, I think of Paymore and Flanigan.

Every company has issues, problems, and weaknesses. The cardinal rule is to *never* share those with your customers or prospects, no matter how close you think you are to them. Our goal as salespeople is to create an atmosphere conducive to making a sale. Mentioning anything negative about your company will doom you to failure, even if it is said as a joke. Perception is reality. Make sure you are creating a positive one.

CHAPTER 32

WHAT TYPE OF IMPRESSION ARE YOU CREATING?

My belief is you have one chance to make a first impression.
—KEVIN MCCARTHY

Every day we interact with hundreds of people. At the end of each interaction, the other party is left with a positive, negative, or neutral impression.

Many times we are unaware of the impressions we make. Negative impressions are made every day, and we are oblivious. Our reputations are built on these interactions.

One of the biggest reasons why negative impressions are made is not being in the moment. Multitasking is a relationship killer. We can't multitask and be in the moment at the same time (my wife reminds me of this constantly).

When we are fully engaged in the moment, our chances of leaving a positive impression increase dramatically. It shows that we care about what the other person is saying.

A hard-and-fast rule is to put your electronic device away whenever you are conversing with someone. Being distracted by your smartphone is rude and inconsiderate of the other person. This should be obvious, but many people do it. It makes who you are talking with feel like what he or she is saying doesn't matter.

One of the most important things we can do in our lives is to make others feel like they matter.

Hundreds of times a day, we have the opportunity to make a difference in someone's day or life. A smile or a kind word can go a long way toward making someone feel good.

CHAPTER 33

It's Not What You Say but How You Say It That Matters

Words can inspire and words can destroy. Choose yours carefully.
—Robin Sharma

When my wife and I walked into a restaurant, there was a sign on the hostess stand that read "5% discount for cash." At first I thought that was a pretty good deal, and then I wondered what would happen if the sign read "5% additional charge for credit cards." How would people react?

It's not what you say but how you say it that makes all the difference. In sales, just as in life, we have a series of interactions with other people, and how we say things matters. It can be the difference between working out a deal and blowing a deal, making someone feel good about him- or herself or really bad about him- or herself. Sometimes just one word is all it takes.

I was with a friend who has a very energetic five-year-old, who was running up and down the hallway with his shoe untied. His father said, "Come over here so I can tie your shoe so you don't fall." The child completely ignored his request and kept running up and down the hall.

The next time he stopped, I said, “If you tie your shoe you will be able to run faster.” Immediately the boy went to his father and got his shoe tied. We both made the same request, but the child didn’t care about falling; he did care about running faster. There was a clear benefit for the child to stop and get his shoe tied, so he did.

Just like in the restaurant, there was a positive benefit for the person to act. Each day, if you choose your words carefully, you will find that you will be a far more effective person in your work and in your life. They key is to slow down and think before speaking. Choosing your words carefully will make all the difference between success and failure.

CHAPTER 34

DO YOU KNOW WHO I AM?

A man wrapped up in himself makes a very small parcel.
—JOHN RUSKIN

I was in San Diego for a business conference. As I stepped up to the front desk to check in, I noticed a woman to my right complaining about something. She was trying to get a room with a king-size bed. As she continued to complain about why she couldn't have this, she wasn't very kind to the front-desk clerk who was trying to help her. At that moment, I decided to give her my room with a king-size bed. I felt that it must be really important for this person to have such a room given the fuss she was making.

I let the front desk know, and they informed the woman next to me, who gave me a halfhearted thank-you. As my attention went back to checking in, I heard the complaining continue, this time about the price of the room. She felt entitled to the king room and at the best price. She was giving everyone, including me, the "Do you know who I am?" attitude. I walked away shaking my head and feeling bad for this person, knowing that she'll never be happy. Even though she thought she was important, she set an awful example of leadership because she made everyone trying to help her feel small. Though she got what she wanted, she left a very negative impression with all involved.

A great leader is someone who is always looking for an opportunity to build people up, not tear them down. This allows people to be more willing to give you their all and thus feel valued. As a leader, it is your responsibility to help people rise above their current places in life. It is to inspire them to strive for greatness.

To get to the top of any profession, you must check your ego at the door. Otherwise, you will have accumulated a bunch of meaningless stuff on the backs of other people. That's not a great place to be.

If you are a "Do you know who I am?" person, it's not too late to change. Each day we have a new opportunity to start over and change who we are. I promise that if you put your ego aside and start respecting people, they will respond immediately. You will be elevated to a place you never thought you could attain.

CHAPTER 35

BALANCING TECHNOLOGY AND THE PERSONAL TOUCH

The more interested you are the more interesting you become.
—BILL ALLEN

As technology advances, it's important to keep the personal touch. Every day we make choices that can be seen as impersonal and that can have an adverse effect on our relationships, sales, and successes. Here are five ways to keep the personal touch in this age of technology.

1. Use pen and paper.

There is nothing better than receiving a handwritten note. As e-mails and texting have become the norm, using handwritten notes can be a very effective way to help you stand out from the crowd.

2. Answer the phone.

Nothing is more frustrating than calling a person or a company and getting an automated voice system. First impressions are everything. Because most companies are now using automated systems, answering the phone will make a big first impression.

3. Give a real present.

Gift cards have become an easy way to give gifts. A thoughtful gift is a much better way to show how much you care about someone.

4. Communicate in the most personal way possible.

It is so easy today to send a text or an e-mail. When you have a choice, always select the most personal way to communicate. Pick up the phone instead of e-mailing or texting. Even better, communicate face-to-face. It will make all the difference if you communicate in a personal way.

5. Be in the moment.

While in a conversation, put down your electronic device. It is rude and annoying when you are talking with someone who is looking at his or her smartphone. Turn it off or put it away. Nothing is more important than the conversation at hand. Because we can only focus on one task at a time, focus on the person in front of you.

The people and companies who are able to balance technology and the personal touch have a huge advantage in this age. Sometimes you have to take an older approach to be on the cutting edge.

CHAPTER 36

FIVE WAYS ARTIFICIAL INTELLIGENCE WILL CHANGE OUR WORLD

Success in creating AI would be the biggest event in human history. Unfortunately, it might also be the last, unless we learn how to avoid the risks.
—STEPHEN HAWKING

My wife and I were out shopping for Christmas presents and decided to eat at a chain restaurant. To our surprise, there was a tablet device at each table through which we could play games, order drinks, call the waitress, and eventually pay our bill. We joked about how one day this device would be our waitress. The next obvious question is, how long will it take?

As artificial intelligence (AI) advances, here are five ways our world will change dramatically.

1. AI Servers

Imagine walking into a fast-food restaurant and ordering by tablet. You don't have to imagine too hard because many places have already introduced these systems. You walk up, punch in your order, and voilà—your number is called, and your food arrives. AI isn't in the picture yet, but what it will bring is a robot that interacts with you. The conversation may go like this:

- AI: "Good morning, Michael. I see you're in a good mood today."
- Mike: "Hello, AI. You are right; I am in a good mood. I would like to order lunch."
- AI: "Great. I have some suggestions for you based on your likes and the fact that you have 28.5 minutes to get back to your next meeting."

Do you see where this is going? Not only will AI be able to tell your mood, but it will also have access to unlimited data about you, including your likes and dislikes and even your schedule for the day. Your experience will be completely customized. It's a bit creepy, I admit, but it doesn't take much to see how it can happen. Just look at all of the personal information available online that we willfully put out there that will be available to an AI. They will know us better than we know ourselves.

2. AI Buyers and Sellers

You walk into a meeting with your largest customer and are greeted by the "new purchasing agent." Your customer has just put an AI purchasing system into place. You get a sinking feeling as the system is being explained to you. You learn how the AI system buys without emotion and makes decisions based on data and analytics. The system knows your costs, fill rates, errors, and so on. And it will analyze your performance versus the competition. After the meeting, you report back to your company what just happened. Before long, your CEO introduces you to the new AI salesperson and announces that the AI will be taking over the largest account at the request of the customer. "We will be much more valuable to our customer if the systems can speak to each other," says the CEO.

3. AI Checkouts

Automated checkout is nothing new. We currently see it at some grocery and big box stores. I have used it when I didn't feel like waiting in line. In the future, it will be much different. Using radio-frequency identification technology, we will walk into the store, swipe our credit card, and then fill our cart with everything we need. Near the door will be a station where our purchase total appears. We will approve it and walk out of the store. All of the items in the cart will be scanned automatically.

4. AI Pharmacies

As you walk into your local drugstore, you are greeted by a robot that asks for you to place your hand into the machine and then scan your prescription. You watch in amazement as the machine fills your order in about two minutes. Since your credit card information will be on file you will be on your way in no time.

5. AI Transportation

You walk up to your car, which is already running, and it greets you and states that you are on time for your 9:00 a.m. meeting. You prepare for the meeting as the car takes you to your destination without any input from you.

These are just five examples of how life will change. When AI takes over, every part of our lives will be different. Think about when the E-ZPass was introduced. It was slow to catch on, and the toll takers were furious because they could see where it was going. I remember driving through a toll and asking for a brochure on the E-ZPass. The toll taker angrily refused to give me one. As more people got them and more E-ZPass lanes were added, the people who didn't have an E-ZPass would have to wait in long lines while the ones who did zipped right through. Now it is becoming commonplace to use this device because it is so convenient. The result is that toll takers are being eliminated. It will be the same with AI. Our participation will determine how quickly AI will be deployed, but it will be deployed and the role of humans will change. The questions we can't answer are "How long will it take?" and "What will we as humans do to stay relevant?"

CHAPTER 37

What You Allow Into Your World Is What You Become

Watch your thoughts; for they become words.
Watch your words; for they become actions.
Watch your actions; for they become habits.
Watch you habits; for they become character.
Watch your character; for it becomes your destiny.
—Lao Tzu

When our kids were younger, we were always very careful who we allowed them to hang around with. We have all heard it many times: "Who you surround yourself with is who you will become." It is a proven fact. And it's not just who but what we allow into our lives that matters. This applies to us as adults just as well. Have you taken note of what you are allowing into your world?

Twenty-Four-Hour News

My wife and I recently stopped watching the twenty-four-hour news programs; we stopped allowing them into our world. It is the best decision we ever made. We were tired of the media taking a story about, say, a school shooting, which is a tragic event, and turning it into a twenty-four-hour-a-day thrashing of every minute detail they could scrape up. What do you think the result is when you watch an event like that for hours on end? It's not happiness.

Just the Facts

However, this is not to say that we are ignorant. We continue to keep up with local and national events, but our policy is "Just give us the facts once." We don't need to know every detail. When there is a new development, give us the facts, and then we move on.

Talk Radio

As a traveling salesperson, I drive forty thousand or more miles per year, so I listen to the radio a lot. I once was a huge talk-radio listener, but no more. Once in a while I will tune in, and what I find with many hosts is a bunch of ranting about how awful everything has become, and this raving feeds off the twenty-four-hour news cycle. Again, what will your frame of mind be when it is filled up with hours of anger, ranting, and raving? Would you say it will be positive?

Have You Noticed?

Have you noticed how sad and angry people are in today's world? I challenge you to pull your face out of your smartphones and take notice. You will see that people are sad, mad, or just plain depressed. And of course they are—look what they are allowing into their lives. Here is another challenge: when you see someone who is happy, strike up a conversation with him or her and find out why.

FIPS: Face-in-Phone Syndrome

I must admit this is a hard one for me, but I am trying to minimize the time I spend with my face in the phone. Have you ever gone out to dinner and seen a family in which each member has his or her face in the phone and there is no conversation going on? It is the hardest to watch when a parent is having dinner with a young child and completely ignoring him or her because something is much more important on Facebook.

Toxic People

Who is in your circle of friends? The rule of thumb is that you always want to associate with people who inspire and encourage you to be better and reach higher. Minimize those "friends" who drag you down, put you in a sour mood, or make you sad or depressed. I'm not saying to ignore friends and family who themselves are depressed or sad and need your help cheering them up, but distance yourself from people who intentionally try to drag you down in an attempt to make themselves feel better. There is a difference between trying to help and inspire people to be better and having them in your circle of influence.

A Problem Identified

Jack Stanley said, "A problem identified is a problem half solved," and that applies here. Awareness is the first step to solving a problem. If people stop watching and listening to the garbage on their TVs, radios, and phones, the networks will take the programming off the air. The big secret is that we are in control of what we allow into our world. When friends ask why you are not hanging around any longer, you will have an opportunity to help them to change.

We ultimately have the choice to either control what comes into our lives or to be controlled by it. We can be leaders who inspire people to reach higher or to be dragged into the ditch of negativity. We can have a salmon mentality or go along with the crowd. The choice is yours.

CHAPTER 38

Why the Millennials Will be the Next Greatest Generation

Millennials are often portrayed as apathetic, disinterested, tuned out, and selfish. None of those adjectives describe the Millennials I've been privileged to meet and work with.
—Chelsea Clinton

The Millennial generation, otherwise known as "Generation Me," is made up of young professionals strapped with college debt, living with their parents, and generally regarded as unmotivated. They are discussed at many conferences, and organizations that can't seem to keep them happily employed are trying to figure them out.

As we are slowly losing the last of the greatest generation, the question is, who will take their place? Certainly not the baby boomers. The baby boomers, my generation, have not done a very good job as stewards. We have racked up massive amounts of debt and are the creators of the shopping mall, suburban sprawl, the North American Free Trade Agreement, and Walmart, to name just a few.

Why the Millennials?

Look at how the millennial generation has already changed our society. They are responsible for the organic and farm-to-table movements, food trucks, and the green and tiny-house movements, as well as a new frugality. They are reviving and moving back to our cities. They are already saving more money than the previous generations, and they are just getting started.

Most employers struggle to understand millennials, and it is important not to misinterpret their motives. Although they may seem distracted and uninterested, they are actually very engaged and observant. What they aren't interested in is the status quo. They come in, look at an organization, and assess the situation very quickly. If they don't see an organization willing to change and move forward, they move on.

Organizations that have trouble retaining millennials are stuck in the past and unwilling to change. Millennials want to make a difference and work their way up the ladder quickly. They aren't satisfied with staying in positions for very long if they aren't being challenged and do not see the opportunity to grow both personally and professionally. If your company isn't looking to grow dramatically and promote quickly, you will have trouble retaining top millennial talent.

This generation grew up with technology and is wired in a different way. They use technology seamlessly and are frustrated very easily if they are working in a company that isn't up to speed. Again, if they don't see where they can make a difference or they don't have the tools to work effectively, they will find a place where they can.

If you take the time to understand the millennial generation and let them help your company change, you will find a group of people who are smart, driven, creative, and confident and who have high integrity. They have everything necessary to become the new greatest generation. It will be exciting to see them continue to grow and blossom.

CHAPTER 39

How Do We Inspire People to Greatness?

Average leaders inspire people to punch a time clock.
Great leaders inspire industry and passion.
—Joseph B. Wirthlin

When writing this chapter, I was planning to focus on the ways leaders demotivate their employees. I wrote out my ideas and then realized that by focusing on what companies are doing wrong, I was perpetuating the exact thing I wanted to help eliminate. Instead, I decided to focus on ways to inspire people to greatness. As leaders, it should be our goal to bring out the best in our employees and the people we influence, to help them become the very best that they can be. We are responsible for training the next generation. I am starting with ten ways to help motivate and inspire people and invite you to add to the list. Together, we can help leaders everywhere to first learn the principles, then to work toward them, and finally to live them.

1. Be a positive example, and do not cultivate a do-as-I-say attitude.
2. Be willing to get your hands dirty when things get tough.
3. Train your employees to their specific needs instead of taking a shotgun training approach.
4. Give praise for a job well done, not for merely existing or for doing mediocre work.

5. Always be open and honest.
6. Have genuine concern for the people you lead.
7. Give full credit for new ideas and reward them instead of criticizing them or taking them for your own benefit.
8. Be a macromanager instead of a micromanager.
9. Encourage communications that are more personal and less electronic.
10. Encourage experimentation versus the status quo, because it's always been done that way.

The goal is to come up with as many great ideas as possible. Get creative. Experiments never fail; the more creative the idea, the better.

CHAPTER 40

DON'T WASTE YOUR TIME

Action is the foundational key to all success.
—PABLO PICASSO

It's my hope that you enjoyed this book.

If you got one good tip from this book and incorporated it into your life, it will make a difference. We grow incrementally, step by step, and every time you change course, it yields fruit.

On the other hand, if you read this book and came away with some good tips but do nothing to implement them, you will have wasted your time, and that would be a shame.

Action is the key to all success. Without it, nothing happens. My last tip is to take action on a regular basis. If you do, you will grow; if you don't, you will wish you did.

Don't grow old feeling regretful that you didn't do all you could to live up to your potential. We get only one shot at this life. Give it your best, and you will have no regrets.

Aspire to reach higher. Your time is right now, because tomorrow is but a wish. Start living your dream today.

Closing

I hope as you finish this book that you have gained some knowledge and insight to help you become a better salesperson and—more importantly—a better person. We have an amazing opportunity to make a difference each day with everyone we meet, to help make others' days a little better and in turn make our lives more fulfilling. The key to joy and happiness in this life is to help others to be happier in small ways, every chance we get.

I leave you with a short summary of each chapter that you can refer to as a refresher.

Thank you so much for reading my book. I am truly honored that you've spent a part of your life reading it. I hope it made a positive impact.

All the best,

Mike

Chapter 1: The key to greatness is selflessness.

Chapter 2: No matter how hard it gets, never give up!

Chapter 3: The only thing we truly own is the day in which we are living.

Chapter 4: Small improvements made over time yield big results.

Chapter 5: There is nothing more important than being kind to our fellow human.

Chapter 6: Success is not defined by what we acquire but by what we give back.

Chapter 7: Where you are right now is your best opportunity to make a difference.

Chapter 8: "A person's a person, no matter how small."—Dr. Seuss

Chapter 9: "Always be a first rate version of yourself, not a second rate version of someone else."—Judy Garland

Chapter 10: Your success in sales has as much to do about your team as it does your skill

Chapter 11: Before looking to blame someone or something for your circumstances, try improving yourself first.

Chapter 12: "Success is neither magical nor mysterious. Success is the natural consequence of consistently applying the basic fundamentals."—Jim Rohn

Chapter 13: "Working smart means wringing maximum production from your work schedule. It's coming up with new ideas to bring that about."—Robert Terson

Chapter 14: "You have to learn the rules of the game. And then you have to play better than anyone else."—Albert Einstein

Chapter 15: The economy is an excuse for you not to grow.

Chapter 16: If you continue to focus on excellence, you won't have to worry about the competition.

Chapter 17: Creativity backed by confidence plus the proper fit will equal a profitable sale.

Chapter 18: "An idea that is developed and put into action is more important than an idea that exists only as an idea."—Edward de Bono

Chapter 19: "In your neediness you repel, in your completeness you attract."—Esther Hicks

Chapter 20: The way we price our products and services has a direct influence on the perception of their value in the customer's mind.

Chapter 21: If you help customers be successful, the price will become less important.

Chapter 22: "One of the most important keys to success is having the discipline to do what you know you should do, even when you don't feel like doing it."—Todd Smith

Chapter 23: "You can have everything in life you want, if you will just help enough other people get what they want."—Zig Ziglar

Chapter 24: Always be realistic in setting a customer's expectations, even if it means losing a sale.

Chapter 25: Selling is a team effort. Thank your team today.

Chapter 26: Defending your territory is just as important as opening new business.

Chapter 27: If you wouldn't buy from a prospect, you shouldn't sell to them either.

Chapter 28: "The bitterness of poor quality remains long after the sweetness of low price is forgotten."—Benjamin Franklin

Chapter 29: "Anyone can sell product by dropping their prices, but it does not breed loyalty."—Simon Sinek

Chapter 30: Never ever take a customer's business for granted, or you will have one foot on a banana peel on your way out the door.

Chapter 31: You are always selling, whether you know it or not.

Chapter 32: You catch more flies with honey than vinegar.

Chapter 33: Words are the most powerful thing we possess. Use them carefully.

Chapter 34: "There is nothing noble in being superior to your fellow man; true nobility is being superior to your former self."—Ernest Hemingway

Chapter 35: There is nothing more important that the person you are interacting with at any given moment.

Chapter 36: Keeping up with technology will allow you to remain relevant.

Chapter 37: You have full control over what you allow into your life. Keep it positive.

Chapter 38: Respect and embrace the millennial generation. You may be working for them someday.

Chapter 39: Inspiring people to greatness will always yield more fruit than tearing them down.

Chapter 40: Start living your dream right now, this very minute!

Recommended Reading and Listening

These are some of the books that have shaped my life and career.

The Holy Bible

Lead the Field
Earl Nightingale

The Magic of Thinking BIG
David Schwartz

The Max Strategy
Dale Dauten

80/20 Principle
Richard Koch

Selling the Invisible
Harry Beckwith

Start with No
Jim Camp

Attracting Perfect Customers
Stacy Hall and Jan Brogniez

Who Moved My Cheese?
Spencer Johnson

Fish!
Stephen C. Lundin and Harry Paul

59951496R00067

Made in the USA
Charleston, SC
19 August 2016